T0012147

DALE EARNHARDT JR.

KENNY ABDO

Fly!

An Imprint of Abdo Zoom

abdobooks.com

abdobooks.com

Published by Abdo Zoom, a division of ABDO, P.O. Box 398166, Minneapolis, Minnesota 55439. Copyright © 2022 by Abdo Consulting Group, Inc. International copyrights reserved in all countries. No part of this book may be reproduced in any form without written permission from the publisher. Fly!™ is a trademark and logo of Abdo Zoom.

Printed in the United States of America, North Mankato, Minnesota.
102021
012022

THIS BOOK CONTAINS RECYCLED MATERIALS

Photo Credits: Alamy, AP Images, Getty Images, iStock, Icon Sportswire, Shutterstock
Production Contributors: Kenny Abdo, Jennie Forsberg, Grace Hansen
Design Contributors: Candice Keimig, Neil Klinepier

Library of Congress Control Number: 2021940205

Publisher's Cataloging-in-Publication Data

Names: Abdo, Kenny, author.
Title: Dale Earnhardt Jr. / by Kenny Abdo
Description: Minneapolis, Minnesota : Abdo Zoom, 2022 | Series: NASCAR
     biographies | Includes online resources and index.
Identifiers: ISBN 9781098226794 (lib. bdg.) | ISBN 9781644946824 (pbk.) |
     ISBN 9781098227630 (ebook) | ISBN 9781098228057 (Read-to-Me ebook)
Subjects: LCSH: Earnhardt, Dale, Jr.--Juvenile literature. | Automobile racing drivers-
     Biography--Juvenile literature. | Stock car drivers--Biography--Juvenile literature. |
     NASCAR (Association)--Juvenile literature. | Stock car racing--Juvenile literature.
Classification: DDC 796.72092--dc23

TABLE OF CONTENTS

DALE EARNHARDT JR.

Following a long family racing **legacy**, Dale Earnhardt Jr. has forged a path of his own.

With multiple **Cup Series** wins and two **Daytona 500** checkered flags, it's clear that racing is in Dale Jr.'s blood.

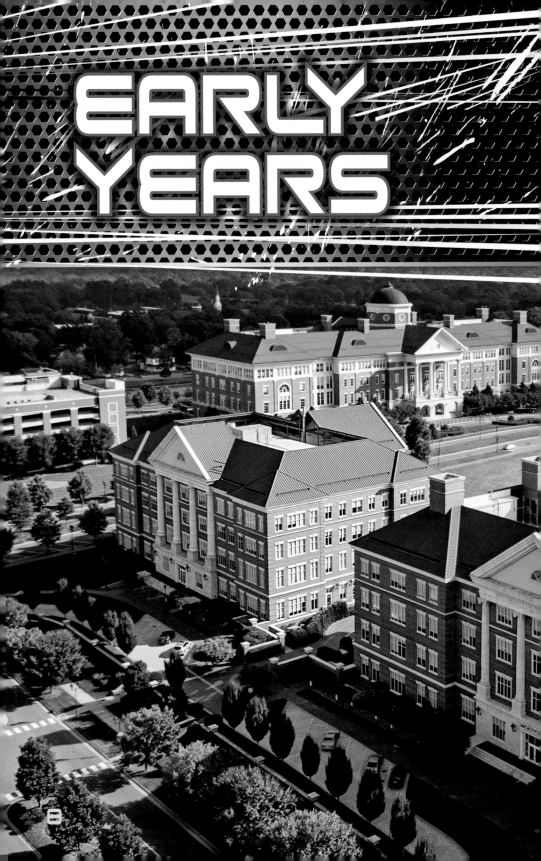

EARLY YEARS

Ralph Dale Earnhardt Jr. was born in Kannapolis, North Carolina, in 1974.

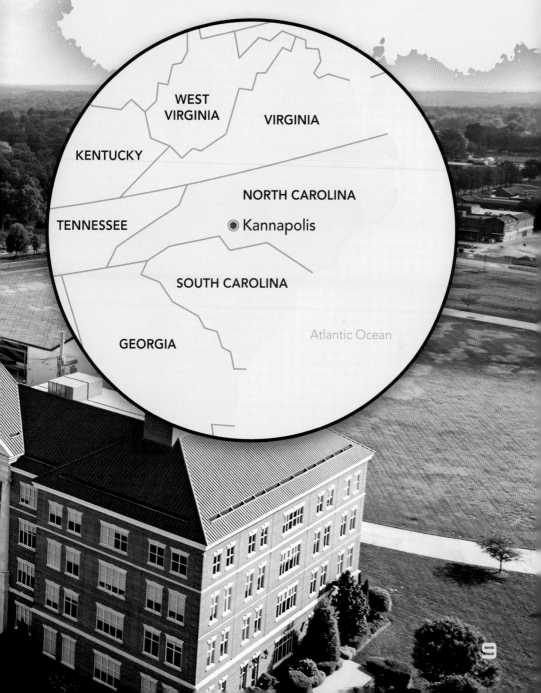

WEST VIRGINIA

VIRGINIA

KENTUCKY

NORTH CAROLINA

TENNESSEE

⊙ Kannapolis

SOUTH CAROLINA

Atlantic Ocean

GEORGIA

Before Dale Jr. started racing, he worked at his dad's car dealership. There, he serviced cars, learning about them inside and out.

Dale Jr. loved cars and learned everything he could about them. At age 17, he and his brother Kerry collected enough money together to buy a 1979 Monte Carlo race car.

THE BIG TIME

In 1996 Dale Jr. got his chance to drive in NASCAR. He drove for his father's team in a few Busch Series races. Dale Jr. got his own **full-time** ride in 1998.

13

Dale Jr. won the NASCAR Busch
Series Championship in his first year!
He won the race again in 1999. In
2000, Dale Jr. became a **full-time**
NASCAR Sprint Cup driver.

Dale Earnhardt Sr. passed away in 2001 after he crashed on the last lap of the **Daytona 500**. Dale Jr. honored his father three years later by winning that race. He did it again in 2014.

In 2015, Dale Jr. won his last **Cup Series** at the Quicken Loans Race for Heroes 500. He scored his last Xfinity Series victory in 2016 at the ToyotaCare 250.

Dale Jr. retired from driving with 24 wins in the Xfinity Series and 26 wins in the **Cup Series**. A total that is tied for 32nd on NASCAR's all-time winners list.

LEGACY

Dale Jr. is known to more than just NASCAR fans. He has been on more than 150 magazine covers, appeared in Hollywood movies, and has even starred in video games!

2016 SEASON PREVIEW

3 of 4 COLLECTOR COVERS

illustrated

NASCAR®

83 Pages Of
→ Profiles
→ Analysis
→ Stats

THE TIME IS RIGHT

2016 Could Be

DALE JR.'S YEAR

STATE OF THE SPORT

In-Depth Look At The NASCAR Landscape

FEB/MARCH 2016

NASCAR.COM/ILLUSTRATED
FACEBOOK.COM/NASCARILLUSTRATED
@NASCARILLUSTR8D

He launched The Dale Jr. Foundation in 2007. The **charity** works to help youths who are in need achieve their goals. Dale Jr. also supports the Make-A-Wish Foundation. He has granted more than 200 wishes while working with them!

Dale Jr. won NASCAR's Most Popular
Driver Award every year from 2003 to
his retirement. He's earned his place
in NASCAR history.

GLOSSARY

charity – an organization set up to provide help and raise money for those in need.

Cup Series – the top racing series of NASCAR where 16 drivers compete for the championship. The first nine races are three rounds, with four participants cut after each.

Daytona 500 – the most famous stock car race in the world and one of the races in the Sprint Cup Series.

full-time – to participate in something on a permanent basis.

legacy – something important or meaningful handed down from previous generations.

ONLINE RESOURCES

Booklinks
NONFICTION NETWORK
FREE! ONLINE NONFICTION RESOURCES

To learn more about Dale Earnhardt Jr., please visit abdobooklinks.com or scan this QR code. These links are routinely monitored and updated to provide the most current information available.

INDEX